Nantucket
Publishing

Also by Harold Morris

Twice Pardoned
Beyond the Barriers
Unshackled

The names and descriptions of many of the people in this book have been changed to protect their identities.

The Law of the Harvest

An inspirational and instructional
guide to help today's teenagers
take charge of their lives.

By Harold Morris

Published by Nantucket Publishing

Published by: Nantucket Publishing
602 S.W. Ward Blvd.
Wilson, N.C. 27893

ISBN Number 0-9662718-1-5

Library of Congress Catalogue Card Number: 98-90158

Manufactured in the United States of America

Jacket Design: Rebecca Lynn; Book Design: Ruth Moore

Editing: Cheves Robinson

Exclusive Distributor To The Trade:

NANTUCKET PUBLISHING
Wilson, N.C.

(For ordering information, please see the final page of this book.)

Introduction

"Welcome to Georgia State Penitentiary," the sign at the entrance made an attempt at a warm greeting.

Hobbling in duck-fashion because of the shackles, I stared up at the massive front gate of the prison.

"How much time have you got, boy?" a prison guard barked.

"Two life sentences," I answered.

"Double elbows! You can forget about it! They're going to carry you out of here in a pine box!"

He pointed with his rifle to a small knoll in the shadow of the towering prison walls. There, hundreds of small white crosses marked the graves of anonymous inmates.

"That's Pissant Hill," he rumbled. "That's where the state sticks your dead body when no one else claims it! You do what I tell you or you will be under the next cross! Now move!"

How could it have all gone so wrong for me? I was only twenty-eight years old, but my life was already over. My head was shaved, I was blasted with a hose, deloused, and given a set of clothes with my prison number stamped across the back.

At 6 p.m., I was locked in a roach-infested cell in M-building. Utterly alone, I broke down in tears. Although I had been found guilty of crimes I did not commit, I realized that night that I had put myself behind bars.

As memories of my former life came flooding back to me I saw how one bad choice had created another. I saw that my life had been an unbroken succession of bad choices that had finally, almost inevitably, landed me in prison. As I lay there on my bunk, lost in loneliness and despair, I wondered why I hadn't understood what seemed so simple and so obvious and so true: I had reaped what I had sown.

What had I sown into my life? I had associated with the worst kinds of people: prostitutes, drug pushers, drug addicts, and ex-convicts. I drank. I did drugs. I had immoral sex. I was proud to call myself a racist.

What did I reap? Two life sentences at Georgia State Penitentiary for armed robbery and murder. And I almost died there.

With the permission of the warden, I began telling my story in high schools throughout south Georgia, trying to keep those young people from making the same mistakes I had made in life. Even though I stood before them in a prison uniform, I wanted to share with them a message of hope and love. I wanted them to know that I loved them and that they could write to me with their personal problems and I would answer their letters.

This book is likewise a message of hope and love. Everyday millions of teenagers and adults live inside prisons just as real as those made of iron bars - the prisons of alcoholism, drug addiction, immorality, despair, racism, poverty, illness and loneliness. I believe that each of these people has the potential to find real happiness in life. We are all born in darkness, and it is up to each of us as individuals to turn on the light.

In sixteen years of public speaking I met many people who found the courage to turn on the light in their lives, and this book is filled with their uplifting stories. But this book is also filled with tragic stories of those who tried to compromise with sin and found, too late, that they could not.

Throughout chapters on wrong association and peer pressure, alcohol, drugs, sex and dating, suicide, race, and love, are unforgettable characters with unforgettable stories. Each and every chapter bears out the same eternal truth - the law of the harvest - you always reap what you sow in life.

HAROLD MORRIS SPEAKS TO PARENTS AND TEENS ABOUT THE LAW OF THE HARVEST

The Law of the Harvest

There is a law that God has written into the physical universe and the spiritual universe, and this is the law: you always reap what you sow in life. If I want to pick tomatoes three months from now, then I have to plant tomatoes. I can't plant something else and expect to get tomatoes. That's the law of the harvest.

The law of the harvest says this: you reap what you sow, you reap later than you sow, but you always reap more than you sow. By planting a tiny acorn you can grow a mighty oak. Now, the law of the harvest applies to the spiritual universe as well as the physical universe. If you plant one evil seed, you will reap evil a thousand-fold in return. And if you plant one good seed, you will reap good a thousand-fold in return. But you always reap what you sow.

You can't sow disrespect, hatred, ignorance, dishonesty, and racism, and expect to reap honor, love, wisdom, truth, and understanding.

Young people, I don't know what kind of life you want, but whatever kind of life you want, pick it out right now. You see, every day you can sow good or evil in your life. You have to choose. And if you are not careful, some of the things you choose to do today can cause you a terrible heartache tomorrow.

I am a perfect example of this. What did I sow into my life? I associated with the wrong kinds of people, I drank,

I did drugs, I had immoral sex, and I was proud to call myself a racist. What did I reap? Two life sentences at Georgia State Penitentiary for armed robbery and murder. And I almost died there.

Growing up in South Carolina, I was an all-state athlete in high school. I captained the football team, the basketball team, and the baseball team. I had numerous scholarship offers, but I couldn't accept them because of my poor grades. So I said, "I'm not going to college. I'm going to drink beer, chase girls - that's the life." I began to go to nightclubs, and in there I consorted with all of the worst kinds of people: prostitutes, drug pushers, drug addicts, ex-convicts - you name it, they were there. And, young people, it took me one year to destroy my life. One year.

I met two men in a nightclub. I envied their fancy clothes and free-spending ways. It seemed to me that they lived life in the fast lane, and I wanted to be a part of that so I became friends with them. We decided to go to Atlanta, Georgia - where I now live - to party, to smoke dope, and have fun. We hit all the night scenes for one week. We checked out of the motel to go back to North Carolina, but before we left my friends wanted to go by and visit these girls that we had met. So, we drove to their apartment complex, but the girls weren't there. My two friends left my car and went a block and a half down the street and decided to rob a supermarket.

They pulled guns on twelve people and told the manager to open the safe. He was getting ready to do that when an innocent bystander pulled a pistol out of his belt to shoot them - to become a hero. But one of them shot him first. And they ran back to where I was, a block and a half away, and they said, "Drive! Drive! We've shot a man!"

The worst mistake I've ever made in my life was driving them back to North Carolina. En route, I asked them what happened, and they told me.

I asked, "Well, did you kill the man?"

They said, "No, he was standing when we left. We're sure he'll be all right."

When they got out of my car, I didn't see them again for one year. In the meanwhile, I was arrested by the F.B.I. They charged me with armed robbery and murder. I learned that the man who'd been shot had died five minutes later.

I was driven back to Atlanta where I went on trial for my life. The district attorney promised he'd see me fry in the electric chair. You see, the district attorney had cut a deal with my two so-called friends, and they agreed to testify against me. They came into that courtroom and took the witness stand and told the jury that I had masterminded the whole crime. After my conviction, they were set free. I was given two life sentences but spared the electric chair.

Lying in a lonely prison cell at Georgia State Penitentiary, I reflected on the events that had led me to such a horrible place. And I cried that night as I thought of my wasted life.

It became clear to me that my problems really began at an early age. In retrospect, I saw that I had always run with the wrong kinds of people, and this had led to an immoral lifestyle fueled by drinking and, later, drugs. My life had been going downhill for a long time, and it wasn't hard to see how each choice I made in life had led me further and further down until I finally hit bottom - Georgia State Penitentiary.

Through that long night of relived memories, I came to understand the law of the harvest, even though I did not call it that then. Although I had been wrongly convicted, I realized that I had put myself behind bars.

I made it out of Georgia State Penitentiary after more than nine years, but the next person I would like to tell you about did not. His story also illustrates the importance of making the right choices in life. Randy Adams died young, but he still lives in my memory and I will never forget him.

On Christmas Day 1974, I promised all the inmates that if I were ever released I would return one day to give everybody there a real Christmas! I never forgot that pledge. Eight years and nine months after my release, along with eighteen of my loyal friends, I returned to Georgia State Penitentiary to fulfill my promise. We had over twenty-five thousand dollars worth of gifts with us - a gift for every inmate in the prison.

At 8:00 p.m., after all the gifts were handed out, my friends gathered in the prison rotunda before departing. As we were about to load up the vans, one of my friends handed me a note that an inmate had slipped to him earlier in the day. The name on it nearly took my breath away: Randy Adams. I hadn't seen him in sixteen years.

I went straight to the warden and said, "Everybody's got to wait. I must go back and see this man."

A deputy warden escorted me back to the prison block.

"You know how old Randy was when I first met him?" I asked. "Fourteen. I was in the county jail, and they put him in there with all the murderers, thieves, rapists and drug addicts. I tried to protect him."

"He's in pretty bad shape," the deputy warden said.

Finally, at the end of the long hallway, the deputy warden stopped and unlocked a cell door. Inside was a man who looked weathered. He took a good look at me and then hobbled over and threw his arms around my neck.

"I knew it was you!" he said in a voice choked with emotion. "I just knew it was you! If you only knew how many times I've thought of you and wondered what happened to you. After all these years . . ." he said, his voice trailing off.

"Randy Adams," I said, holding him at arm's length. "Let me get a good look at you."

The last time I'd seen him he was a pimple-faced fourteen-year-old kid. Sixteen years later, his face was prematurely wrinkled and covered with scars, and there were streaks of gray through his tangled mop of mud-brown hair.

Randy was about six-foot-two and skinny as one of the bars in his cell door. Every exposed part of his body had slash marks. Some had healed, others had festered. On his bony wrists were scars, obviously recent. He looked filthy and smelled like old hamburger.

I asked the deputy warden if we could meet privately, and he ushered us into a nearby holding room just outside the cell block, locking me in with Randy. During our short walk, I noticed that Randy hobbled badly on his right foot and dragged his left leg. I asked what the problem was.

"Leg's been amputated just below the hip," he answered. "Got infected from a dirty needle."

"How about your right foot, what's wrong with it?"

"Part of my toes are missing."

As I sat looking at him, I remembered him as a scared kid acting tough in a county jail. It was a terrifying place for a youngster, and I tried to help him. But he wouldn't listen to my advice. One night in a fit of anger, he'd stabbed me with a fountain pen. But most of the time he respected me, and I became his protector. I didn't see him again after I was shipped to Georgia State Penitentiary.

"Randy, tell me what happened in your life since we were together," I said.

"Got raped right after you were transferred," he said. "Wanted to kill the sorry convict, but then I got released. That was all right, being out again, but it didn't last long. In Florida I stole a car, and then I robbed a bank and did time in a Florida state pen for several years. Got released again and came back to Georgia, but they busted me for drugs and . . . well, here I am. The guards, they've shot me four times trying to escape. Now I got diabetes, and I'm going blind. They don't give me a long time to live."

"Randy, how about the slash marks?" I asked.

"I put some of them there. Others were from fights."

"What about your throat?" I asked, eyeballing the expansive purple mark that cut from one side of his neck to the other.

"Tried to kill myself. I just couldn't take it anymore." He paused. "You remember the time you took an iron pipe and beat that punk almost to death because he was messing with me? Grabbed that pipe and went after him. You looked after me. You protected me when anybody bothered me."

I felt a twinge of embarrassment when Randy spoke. This was a side of my life that I didn't want resurrected.

Looking at Randy, I felt a lump in my throat. He had a man's body, what was left of it, but in his eyes I saw a scared fourteen-year-old boy who'd never grown up. He was a shell of a man, the perfect picture of a wasted life. If the warden had told me to take Randy home with me, I couldn't have. Randy simply could not have survived on the outside. What could a man do who was missing his left leg and part of his right foot, who was going blind, and was popping all kinds of pills to medicate the last months of his life? Without insurance, who would pay the medical bills? What company would hire him? Where would he live?

But escape was all Randy could think about.

"Harold, you got to help me get out of here," he suddenly pleaded. "I don't want to die here. I don't got long to live, you see. I'd try to go over the fence, but they've already shot me four times. And now I can't even run."

I nodded without saying anything. It was tragic, but I realized that Randy was better off in prison, though I couldn't tell him that. I didn't know what to say.

His eyes studied my face before he finally broke the silence, "Harold, I don't understand. You used to be so full of hate. I remember that."

"Yeah, Randy, I remember that, too," I said.

"But you come here and do something no one has ever done. You give us stuff. You remember us on Christmas."

"I finally learned that hatred is not the answer, Randy."

When I started to leave, Randy threw his arms around me. I could feel the desperation in his fingers as they dug into my shoulders, and he didn't let go for a very long time.

The results of our Christmas visit were better than anything I could have dreamed up in my wildest imaginings. As we drove to a motel for the night, one of my friends handed me a note from an inmate he had visited. The note was brief and to the point: "Harold, thanks for the Christmas gifts. Love, Sly."

I couldn't believe it. "Love, Sly"? It was written plain as day by a man who'd killed at least three people. He was the neighbor who'd snarled to me my first day on death row, "Hey, next door, I'm going to kill you." Somehow in the intervening years, he had changed.

My amazement didn't stop there. A week after our visit, I received a thank-you card signed by 190 inmates. Others wrote individual letters to say that my book gave them new hope. Of course, there were a few con artists who wrote to say they were innocent, too, and asked me to speak to their judge or call their parents or help them find a job or send them money.

The most precious letter was from Randy.

"It's four o'clock in the morning, and I just finished reading your book, *Twice Pardoned*," he wrote. "You will never know what your visit has meant in my life. But I am not going to live long, and I know it. Before I die, I'd just ask one favor. I got a fourteen-year-old nephew who doesn't live far from you. He is on drugs and is going down the same path that led me to prison.

"Please, Harold, don't let him become what I am. He's the same age I was when I got into trouble. In the last sixteen years, I've been outside prison for less than one year. I don't want anybody to have to repeat my life, but I'm afraid he might if something doesn't happen to change things. My sister has done all she can to help him, but he won't listen and they'd never let me speak to him. Please, Harold, help my nephew. Tell him about me - how I ruined my life."

As I read Randy's letter I was heartened to see a man who wanted to reach out and help somebody else. Though his own life was wasted and almost over, he had a burden for another person who was following in his footsteps towards disaster. I did meet with his sister and his nephew and did my best to help him.

We continued to correspond, and I sent him some money and visited him when I could. I thought often about Randy, and how, in a sense, his life represented my work. He is a vivid picture of the toll that alcohol, drugs, and wrong choices can have on a teenager who follows the wrong crowd.

In one letter Randy wrote, "I wish I could do what you are doing. I wish I could tell young people the importance of making the right decisions. I wish they could see my body, all chopped up and scarred, because then they might understand. My life has just been a very long, slow, painful process of dying."

After many discussions, the prison authority transferred Randy to a prison hospital in Milledgeville, Georgia, where he could get better medical attention. On March 17, 1988, fifteen months after my Christmas visit, I received the phone call I had been expecting. Randy had died. I was true to my word and saw that he had a proper burial in a cemetery in Milledgeville. What a tragedy!

Wrong Association and Peer Pressure

A problem that I faced as a teenager, and a problem that teenagers face today is handling peer pressure and dealing with acceptance. Young people will do a lot of things to gain acceptance. Many times they make mistakes to gain acceptance into a group that's not going anywhere and these mistakes hurt them and haunt them for the rest of their lives.

Why do young people crave acceptance? I think it's because many don't like themselves the way they are. They have low self-esteem, and they desperately want the approval of others. They want to be liked and loved more than anything on earth, and the sad thing is many of them will do just about anything in order to gain this approval and acceptance. And it's different with the boys than it is with the girls.

One of the ways the guys gain acceptance is through material possessions. You have seen the guy in the flashy clothes, the fancy car. He wants the attention of others, and he'll do anything to get it. But what he doesn't know is that anyone who accepts him just because of his material possessions, because of what he owns, is not really his friend. Don't be fooled into believing that you can buy someone's friendship with material possessions. Those people who pretend to be your friends are playing you for a sucker, because they're more interested in what you have than who you are.

Some boys will turn to athletics to gain acceptance. That was the route I chose. Now, athletics are good. They've meant a lot in my life. I think athletics teach character. But athletics are not the most important thing. Being a good student academically is far more important. I look at my life today, and I realize that even though I excelled on the athletic field, I would have done better to excel in the classroom. When I was in school I was always prepared for the next ball game, but I never studied and prepared myself for the game of life, and that's the most important game of all.

Other boys will pull the chair out from under someone or put chewing gum in the teacher's chair to get a laugh. Still other boys will brag about how great they are and all the exciting things they've done, but, in reality, they haven't done anything. And finally, there are the boys who will drink the booze, smoke the dope, do other drugs, pop the pills, and smoke the cigarettes. All of these boys have one thing in common: they desperately want the attention and the approval of others.

But you stay away from the boys who get mixed up in alcohol and drugs, because they are on the same path I chose as a youngster. They're headed for trouble and possibly for prison.

With the girls, it is totally different. To girls, beauty is the most important thing. Appearance is so important. I think it's partly because our society has put a premium on physical attractiveness. And the number one problem girls have is keeping up with that girl who gets all the attention, all the dates.

Well, let me tell you about her: because of all the attention and all the pressure she's under, many times she'll get married at an early age. She won't go to college. She will have one child after another, and she stands a greater chance of her marriage ending in divorce. When you see her coming down the street she's got a cigarette hanging in her mouth and so much make-up all over her face that you could write your name in it. And she is miserable. You'll say, "Look at that hag."

Now, when I was in high school I was the meanest student there. One day I told this girl, I said, "You ugly."

And she looked at me and she said, "Well, beauty is only skin deep."

And I said, "Honey, with you, ugly goes all the way to the bone."

She was so ugly her boyfriend took her to the beach and the waves wouldn't come in. Not only was she ugly, she was skinny. She was so skinny she got a run in her panty hose and fell through the hole. She could stand sideways and stick out her tongue, and she looked like a zipper. She was so skinny she could stand under a clothesline and not get wet.

One of my friends said to me one day, "Be nice to her, Harold, look up her family tree, it will tell you a lot about her."

"Look it up?" I responded. "It looks like it fell on her."

I just saw that same girl not too long ago, and you know what she said? She said, "You're right. Ugly does go all the way to the bone. I'm looking at you!"

But let me tell you about her today. She's married, has two kids, and today she's beautiful. You know why? She always had a beautiful personality. She had character. She cared about her appearance. She always dressed well. She went to college and got a good education so she wouldn't have to depend on some sorry guy to support her. And she had compassion for others. To me she is indeed beautiful. So that equation, beauty equals happiness, does not always prove to be true.

Right now you may think that group acceptance is the most important thing in your life. But the most important thing you can do as a young man or a young woman is to stand up for what you believe in and not be swayed by peer pressure. Be a leader in your school, and you will give others courage to resist peer pressure.

Young people, never sacrifice your ideals or your potential to gain acceptance in a group that's not going somewhere. You can belong to the right group if you'll choose one that has the same ideals and the same goals as you have. But don't follow the wrong crowd.

How do you resist peer pressure? I'll tell you how: first of all, you be selective in who you associate with. You choose a group that's going somewhere. I promise you, if you choose the wrong group it will determine the outcome of your life, good or bad.

And secondly, take a stand and learn how to say a simple, two-letter word: "n-o".

Some of you have a problem learning to say no to those things that you know are wrong. If your friends shun you because you stand for what you believe in then they weren't really your friends.

At Georgia State Penitentiary I decided to quit doing drugs. One day two of my friends came up to me at my bunk and said, "Hey, man, you wanna smoke some dope?"

And I said, "I'm through."

They said, "Yeah, you'll be back."

For the first time I had taken a stand. I had said, "No." They left me alone after that, and if you'll learn to say no those that are trying to pull you in the wrong direction will leave you alone, too.

Thirdly, if you want to resist peer pressure, you must count the cost. Think things through. Ask yourself, "What happens if I give in and do this?" Even little things like cheating on a test or telling a lie can have unintended consequences. Remember, you always reap what you sow.

Young people, wrong association is so important. I'm living proof. One night of pleasure almost wrecked my life. But I was given another chance at life, and I'm so thankful for that.

Alcohol

Where did it begin for me? I began drinking alcohol as a sophomore in high school. When I got drunk for the first time I was with two seniors at a house party on the beach. They handed me a vodka bottle and said, "Take a drink."

I knew it was wrong, but I drank it. It was the most awful stuff I'd ever tasted in my life. I turned around and threw up. But when they passed it around again, I took another drink. Why? Because I wanted to be accepted. I wanted them to like me and think I was really a cool guy.

You see, I had low self-esteem. I didn't like myself or my family. I was ashamed of how poor we were. I was ashamed of the old run down shack we lived in and the fact that my father couldn't read or write. He had never been to school a day in his life. All I wanted was to be accepted and loved by everybody.

I drank throughout high school and later in college. I said, "Man, this is the thing to do." I always justified my drinking by saying "everybody's doing it". But everybody wasn't doing it then, and everybody isn't doing it now. That's just a cop-out.

Young people, I've been right where you are today, and I can tell you from experience that alcohol will wreck your life. So, why do so many teenagers drink alcohol? First of all, I think society promotes teenage drinking. All you have to do is turn on the television, and you will see some great athlete with a beer in his hand trying to entice you to drink alcohol. He would have you think that drinking alcohol gave him that tremendous body that God gave him. He is promoting drinking alcohol for the almighty dollar and no other reason. But he will never tell you about the dangers of drinking.

I was speaking in a school in Georgia one day, and I saw a teenage boy in a wheelchair in the front row start crying as I began to tell about the dangers of alcohol.

Later I asked one of the coaches, "What's wrong with him?"

He said, "Last year, under the influence of alcohol, he was out speeding in an automobile. There was an accident. His young friend was killed, and he's to be paralyzed for the rest of his life. He's one of the greatest athletes ever to attend this school. But he's through. Because of alcohol, he has wiped out his potential."

Another reason teenagers drink is that, frankly, their own parents promote it. A teenage boy once explained to me why he didn't feel there was anything wrong with him drinking alcohol or smoking cigarettes.

"You see, my dad drinks and smokes, and he told me, 'It's alright, son, to do that.' And so I did. If my dad says it's okay, then it must be okay."

A friend of mine shared an article with me that was in the local newspaper of the town he lived in. Two sixteen-year-old boys went out speeding in an automobile. There was an accident. Both were killed. The highway patrolman that investigated that accident found a liquor bottle in the back seat of the car. He then had the very difficult job of going to the parents and telling them that their sons were dead. At the first home, the father answered the knock on the door.

The patrolman said, "Sir, I regret to inform you, but your son is dead. And, sir, I also regret to inform you, but he was under the influence of alcohol. We found a liquor bottle in the backseat."

The father became hysterical, he raged, "I would kill the man that sold my son alcohol! I would choke him to death with my bare hands!"

The father became so emotional that he went over to the liquor cabinet to get a drink to settle his nerves. He opened the liquor cabinet; there was a note. It read, "Dear Dad, I took a fifth of liquor with me, because I knew you wouldn't mind."

That father had killed his son. That father reaped what he had sowed.

After I spoke in an assembly program in a high school one day, a teenage girl handed me a pack of cigarettes.

"I'm through smoking and drinking alcohol," she said.

"That's great, honey," I said. "I'm glad you won't be spoiling your pretty teeth any longer with those old cigarettes."

Then she handed me her matches.

"Take these," she said. "I'm serious."

"I'm so proud of you. You're taking a stand. Please know that you have the strength, power, and courage to overcome smoking, alcohol, or any other problem you have. And I will do all I can to help you."

It seems smoking cigarettes and drinking alcohol go hand in hand with so many of our young people. I addressed this one day in a high school assembly.

I said, "Now if you were intended to smoke, you would have been born with a little chimney on top of your head, or your nose would have been turned upside down so you'd go like a choo-choo train."

I was speaking one day to a group of people, and after my speech an old lady came up to me. She asked, "Young man, will smoking send you to hell?"

I said, "No, ma'am, but it will make you smell like you have been there."

She just turned and left without saying a word.

Young people, you don't need that garbage in your life. I promise you. You simply must realize how it will affect your health. So what's the answer? Why do so many young people continue to drink and smoke even though they know it is the wrong thing to do? Why do so many teenagers rebel against their parents' authority? I think the missing ingredient in so many homes today is love. And so many parents aren't even aware of it.

Many a father has said to me, "I work hard to make a living for my family. Somebody has to pay the bills. I do everything for my kids. I give them everything. And you're telling me my son is smoking cigarettes, drinking alcohol, and doing drugs. I can't believe this! Our home has love!"

So many parents do their best to share love, but kids see love differently. A new bicycle or a new automobile isn't always love in a kid's eyes. Giving a hug or a kiss, going to the ball game, the park or the zoo - in these a kid sees love.

If a teenager is prepared to stand on his own in a sick, hurting, dying world, it will be because parents have taken time to deal with his problems - taken time, that is, to love!

Young people want something real. They want and need and deserve parents who love them enough to set an example for them. They're looking for role models. They're tired of the double standard: a parent with a beer in one hand and a cigarette in the other preaching, "Do as I say, not as I do."

And then, finally, teenagers drink alcohol because they want to be powerful - to defy their parents, their principals, their teachers, their pastors. "Everyone else is doing it," they say. They want to be cool, powerful and gain acceptance in their little peer groups. Well, everyone isn't doing it.

At Georgia State Penitentiary I would see these young guys come in, and I'd say, "Son, tell me, why are you here?"

Did you know that practically all of them told me that their problems had an alcohol root to them? That's where it begins.

I heard a story about this football coach who wanted to teach his players about the dangers of alcohol. When they were all seated in the locker room, he called Fat up to the front of the room. Now, Fat was a 320 pound offensive lineman, and he lumbered up to where the coach was standing.

"I'm going to do an experiment here, Fat," the coach told him. "And I want you to watch closely. After I'm done I want you to tell your teammates what you have learned. Okay?"

Fat nodded. The coach put a glass on a stool and filled it with pure grain alcohol - 180 proof.

"Are you watching closely, Fat?" the coach asked as he produced an earthworm.

"I'm watching," Fat said, eyeing the glass of alcohol single-mindedly.

The coach dropped the earthworm into the alcohol, and it immediately flipped over on its back and threw its heels up in the air and died - graveyard dead.

"Well, what'd you think of that experiment, Fat?" the coach asked after a long silence during which Fat still wore an expression of studious concentration.

Finally, Fat said, "That's a great experiment, coach. I got a lot out of that!"

"Why don't you turn around and tell the rest of the players exactly what you learned?"

Fat turned around, and he threw out his chest. Wearing a self-satisfied look, he surveyed the faces of his teammates and said, "Now, what I got out of that there experiment is this - if you drink a lot of that there alcohol, you won't never have none of them worms."

After a high school assembly program a teenage boy

came up to me and told me, "My dad would kill me if he knew I smoked dope and drank beer. What you told us is so true. First it's cigarettes, then alcohol, then marijuana and other drugs, and finally sex. Everything you said has happened to me. I want you to know I'm through with that dead-end lifestyle. Thank you, sir, I wish I could have met you a long time ago."

"It's never too late," I told him. "You've learned a valuable lesson. Now, you can help your friends with similar problems. Your whole life is ahead of you. I'm so proud of you! You can make a difference with your life, son. I admire you for taking a stand!"

Drugs

The best way to describe the dangers of drugs would be to share with you about Georgia State Penitentiary and many of the experiences I had there. I have seen men there inject drugs into their veins and develop serious infections from unclean needles. I've seen addicts with amputated arms and legs. I've seen addicts lose their eyesight, their hair, and develop hepatitis - all because of drugs. I watched a nineteen-year-old boy sniff glue out of a bread sack. He went into a coma and became a vegetable. He stayed that way six months until he died. They buried him in the prison graveyard, because no one claimed his body.

When I think of drugs and alcohol, I guess I think of marijuana as well, because marijuana is the second most preferred drug by teenagers. And the great danger about marijuana is you don't know what you're getting when you buy it. You see, you buy it from the drug pusher, and he's the scum of the earth. He would sell his soul for the almighty dollar. In prison we scored some marijuana that had been dipped in opium or some other hallucinogenic drug. It nearly drove us crazy. One inmate attempted suicide.

The most horrible thing I've ever seen in my life happened to a twenty-year-old inmate who slept in the bunk next to mine. I watched two men come up to his bunk and hold him down while a third guy stabbed his eyes out with a knife.

They thought that he had ratted out a drug transaction they were involved in. It was later proven that he was totally innocent.

The next day they said, "Why did we do it? He was our friend."

He is blind today. I promise you that you don't want to mess around with drugs or even associate with those who do. Those people are sowing all of the wrong things into their lives, and they will reap the addiction that leads to desperation and then to crime and eventually to prison.

I would give anything if I could take you to Georgia State Penitentiary and let you spend one day and go through the normal routine that I went through. Then you might have a different outlook on life and might even find it easy to say no to drugs.

There were 3,200 men crammed into a building built for 750. The dormitory where I was housed was built for 45 men, but I was crowded in with 115 of the meanest, most vicious, short-tempered men anywhere in the world - men who had committed every crime conceivable to man. In that dormitory there were two commodes and one shower for 115 men, and I once saw a man killed in an argument over a pair of shower shoes.

Violence is a way of life in prison, and only the strong survive. I must have seen over 50 men die in the nine-and-a-half years I was incarcerated. Do you realize that 85% of the inmates participated in homosexual behavior? That 75% participated in drug use? I promise you, you don't want that kind of life. So, be thankful for your school, your teachers, and your parents.

You may say, "Man, my school is a prison. A dog wouldn't eat the kind of food they serve us."

Let me tell you about a meal that they served us at Georgia State Penitentiary. I ate it for three years, and I liked it until I found out what I was eating. One day my buddy, Doc, was sitting next to me.

He said, "How do you eat that slop?"

I said, "Man, this is good. This is Brunswick stew."

He said, "Oh, it is, huh?"

He reached over in my bowl and said, "What is this?"

And there was an eyeball looking at me. Every Thursday they would chop up hog heads, throw them in these huge vats, throw vegetables in, and call it Brunswick stew.

The next time you eat lunch at school be thankful that you don't have to eat that kind of food, and give thanks for what you have. Young people, you have so much to be thankful for.

After I spoke to a group of high school students, a teenage boy gave me a handful of marijuana leaves used to wrap marijuana joints.

"I'm through with this stuff," he said.

"Where's the marijuana?" I asked.

"In the car."

"Go get it. I won't turn you in," I promised.

Minutes later he returned with the marijuana.

"Now I believe you," I said. "If you hadn't gone after the marijuana, your words wouldn't have meant much."

"I'm through," he repeated. "Thank you, sir. I will never forget you."

I went to the men's room and flushed that junk down the toilet.

How serious are drugs in this country?

I'm convinced that the drug problem in this country is one of the most serious problems this country has ever faced. And we don't seem to be serious about it. A solution must be found very quickly, because drugs are destroying the lives of too many of our nation's young people.

I'm also convinced that the adults that use and sell cocaine and other drugs are aware of the dangers and don't care. We need to take a serious look at cocaine because it's the source of crack, which is at the root of the problem of despair and bloodshed in our inner cities, especially among our young blacks.

How do we stop it? There is no way to keep people from wanting drugs. And we simply can't arrest our way out of it. Locking so many people up isn't the answer.

So what's the answer? We must stop the source, the cartels, the drug lords, those who are responsible for bringing most of the cocaine and other drugs into this country. We must use force. We are a powerful nation, and they are individuals. We have the troops and the manpower to stop them.

They should be arrested, brought to this country, and given a trial. They should be convicted and given the death penalty. In a short period of time, after the first one is put to death, they will be dealing elsewhere. They will take their business to other countries.

We could solve the drug problem in this country in a short period of time if we really wanted to. We have the power to stop them. But we don't have the courage or the guts.

Why is drug abuse so widespread?

I think drug abuse is so widespread in this country because of the desire of the people, because of the variety of drugs that are readily available to us such as cocaine, marijuana, the pills and other drugs, and because drug use is heavily promoted by the media. They seem to glorify legal and illegal drugs. Finally, I think drug abuse is so widespread because society tolerates it.

I would now like to give you some examples that will show you the importance of saying no to drugs.

I was visiting two friends in South Carolina, and I heard them talking about a young boy. He had broken in a drug-store and overdosed in an apparent attempt to kill himself. By pumping out his stomach, they saved his life. He was locked up in the local jail. He came from a wealthy family, but his family had disowned him. He had been in so much trouble that he had been kicked out of every school in the county. I went to that jail, and I asked to see that young boy. They locked him in a small room with me.

He was the most filthy-looking sight I've ever seen — you could smell him as he came up to you. He looked at me, and he said, "Sir, everybody thinks I smoked marijuana, but I've been snorting cocaine since I was thirteen years old. You see, I hate my dad. He gives me the money to buy it. He doesn't care about me. And I'd kill him today if I could get to him. I have no reason to live."

I looked at him, and I said, "Son, I want to tell you something. I don't know your father, but I care about you very much. And I'm going to get you turned over to me for twenty-four hours, and I'm going to take you to Georgia State Penitentiary. I want you to see the place you're going to spend the rest of your life if you continue the lifestyle you're living."

Well, arrangements were made with a judge, and he turned the boy over to me for twenty-four hours. I called the warden, and I asked him if I could see three inmates who were there. I called them the "unholy three."

The first man that came down was Big Head Yank. He had been there 19 years. It was August, and it's extremely hot in south Georgia in August. He had on a sweatshirt. He had a shirt over that. He had on a prison jacket, a prison hat, dark glasses, and a scarf around his neck. And he walked up and said, "Hey, punk, what's your name?"

And the boy almost forgot his name. He said, "M-m-m-m-m-m" and repeated his name.

He said, "Sit down, boy." He looked over at the boy, and he said, "Boy, how old are you?"

He said, "Sevent-teen, sir."

He said, "When I was your age, I'd done come to prison for murder. I done robbed a bank. I rented a motel, filled it up with women, and I've done come here and killed three teenagers just like you, boy."

Big Head Yank reached into his pocket and pulled out three indictments that he had carried around for nineteen years and showed them to the boy. Then, suddenly, the big man barked, "Get off my foot!"

The boy jumped back and piped, "Yes, sir!" even though he wasn't on the inmate's foot.

I called down another inmate, and he looked at this young boy and he said, "Son, I want to tell you about my life. You see, at age ten I killed my mother. I beat her to death with a baseball bat. I've been here twelve years. I've never received a letter. I'll probably never receive one, either. I've never had a visit from anyone. The only friend I have in the world is Harold. I have a life sentence, and I deserve to die in prison. Son, please, you don't want this kind of life. I want you to leave here today and never forget my face or this prison. Please listen to Harold. He cares about you." He turned and walked away.

I had saved the best until last. His name was Big Mac. He had been in prison twenty-four years. He weighed about two hundred-and-fifty pounds. He had tattoos all over him. He had scars from stab wounds all over his body. He was a drug addict. He was a homosexual. He walked up and grabbed the boy and said, "Punk, what's your name?"

The boy forgot his name again.

Big Mac looked at him and said, "Listen to me. I don't like Morris. I never have. And I want you to leave here today, and I want you to go out and I want you to smoke dope, I want you to shoot dope, drink alcohol, I want you to rob, steal and murder. Do it all, son, because then you're coming back here and I'm gonna make you my boy. You're cute."

And Big Mac lifted the boy off the floor, and he kissed him on the mouth. That young boy went crazy, he ran to the door, and said, "Let me out! Let me out!"

They let him out, and all the inmates and the guards were laughing. I was about to crack up myself. I went out

to the car, and he was sitting there. I got in the car, but I
didn't say a word for several moments. Finally, he looked
at me.

With tears in his eyes, he wiped his mouth with his hand
and said, "He kissed me. He's an animal." Then he said,
"Mr. Morris, will you help me? Please, help me."

Well, I went to his family, and together we persuaded the
judge to give him probation under certain conditions. He
was to be tested for drugs once a week, and he was to
continue his education. We got him back in school. Four
years later, I was sitting in my apartment in South
Carolina, there was a knock on the door, and there he
stood.

He hugged my neck, and he said, "Mr. Morris, I'll never
forget that day at Georgia State Penitentiary. And I'll never
forget Big Mac. He kissed me!"

Then he took his hand and wiped his mouth as he
frowned.

"But because of those men that day, my life had
changed," he said. "I will never forget them. I just
wanted you to know that I'm doing well in college, and
I'm thinking about going into the ministry. Thanks for
everything, Mr. Morris."

Drugs will wreck your life, young people, know that.
Drugs are a one way street going nowhere. If you've started,
stop. If you haven't started, don't start. Yes, you reap what
you sow.

Sex and Dating

Many times when I finished speaking in a high school assembly, teachers would invite me to come to their classrooms. I enjoyed talking with kids in a classroom far more than in an assembly. In the gym, many of the kids were embarrassed to ask a question, but in the class they were among friends and felt more freedom to talk about the issues that affected their lives.

"I don't have all the answers," I said after the teacher introduced me and told the kids they could ask whatever they wanted. "I've come here today because I love you, and if you have a problem, you write me or call me collect. We'll work it out together."

I passed out a stack of cards with my name, address, and phone number.

In the first class, a group of giggling girls sat together on one side of the room.

"Will you look at these angels? They must be having a recess in heaven," I quipped. And turning my attention to the girls, I pointed at several boys and said, "Now you stay away from these sorry rascals, hear?"

All the girls started laughing and that naturally sparked a discussion about dating. One of the girls asked a question about sex. "It's like the guys have only one thing on their minds," she said. "And sometimes I wish we could just have a good time without getting, you know, physical and all."

"Honey, the problem with most teenagers is that they wait until they're in the back seat of an automobile to make a decision," I said. "You'll fail every time if you do that. Now girls, let me tell you what to look for with these guys when you're out on a date. See, these sorry rascals will take you out, and they'll park. And he thinks he's a cool dude in the groove. He thinks he's King Cool, and he'll look over at you and say, 'Baby, you know what you are?'

"And you'll say, 'What?'

"He'll say, 'You are a T.F.'

"You'll say, 'What in the world is a T.F.?'

"He'll say, 'You're a total fox.'

"And you'll say, 'Gollee, he's nice.'

"And then he'll look at you, and he'll say, 'Ain't gonna be long before you'll be a U.B.M.'

"And you'll say, 'What in the world is a U.B.M.?'

"He'll say, 'An Ultra Bad Mamma.'

"And you'll say, 'Gollee, he is King Cool. He's so nice.'

"But look out, the sorry rascal is setting you up.

"He'll look at you and say, 'If you love me, prove your love.'

"Listen to me. He doesn't love you. Anyone that'll ask you to prove your love doesn't love you. I used that line many years ago. He's taking you to be the biggest fool, the most gullible fool that ever walked this earth. You figure it out for yourself. What is he asking you to do when he says, 'Prove your love.'?

"He's asking you to commit immoral acts. He's asking you to surrender your virtue, throw away your self-respect, jeopardize your precious reputation, and risk getting pregnant or getting some disease. That's not love. Anyone who loves you wants what's best for you.

"You need to say no to those sorry characters. You see, he doesn't love you, he loves himself and wants to use you.

"Now, he might not ask you out again, but he's doing

you a favor. You don't need a character like that. You see, he's a Romeo. He's a Don Juan. And that's not what you need. You see, all the girls want a macho man. And all the guys want a macha girl. But that's not what you need. You need a natcho man and a natcha girl. That's one who will take a stand and say, 'I'm natcho man' and 'I'm natcha girl with a lot of cheese on it.' These are boys and girls who will stand for what they believe in and never give in.

"So you start looking for a natcho and a natcha. 'Cause let me tell you about that sorry rascal, girls. After he gets what he wants, he'll move on to someone else and brag about his conquest. He doesn't care about you. Please, take a stand and never give in to immoral sex."

Too many girls feel that they have to play the dating game, and many will do anything to get a date. Many will even lower their standards. Please, never never lower your standards to get a date. You will regret it later if you do.

Girls, never be flattered that there are boys willing to use you. Listen, you could dress up as a parking meter and some of these characters would say, "Hey! Baby! What's happening?"

Please, don't look back on your life and say, "If only I had one more chance."

One day I was speaking at a high school assembly in Georgia. After my speech was over, one of the girls who'd sat quietly in the corner came up to me. She started to cry as she said, "I wish I could have heard this two months ago. I really needed it then."

"Well, it's better late than never," I said. I looked at her and asked the question to which I already knew the answer, "Are you pregnant?"

She nodded.

"Have you told anyone?"

"No. My parents would kill me if they found out."

"What's your name, honey?"

"Cynthia."

"Cynthia, there was a time when I thought it was too late for me. But it wasn't. It's never too late."

"I'd just like to get rid of this problem, to have it over with. No one would know."

"Honey, it's not a problem. It's a baby, a human life. I know this is a terribly lonely time for you, and I'm sure it's tempting to think about an abortion. But I hope you'll think not just about your life, but also about the life of the baby inside you.

"Please do me a favor. Tonight would you give this a great deal of thought? Do that, and then I want you to call me collect when we have more time to talk. Cynthia, I want to help you. Just promise you'll call. I'll talk to your parents. I'll stand by you all the way. I give you my word. It's not too late. Together we can work this out. Every day is a new day, and I care about you. You promise to call?"

"I promise."

I followed up with Cynthia. We had many, many phone conversations over the next few months. I even visited her and her parents. Finally, one day I received a letter from her saying she'd followed my advice not to have an abortion. She also stated that she was attending church.

"I want to thank you for loving me and caring," she wrote. "You were so right. That boy who got me pregnant has never spoken to me to this day. In fact, he laughs at me when he sees me. I dropped out of school for a term to have the baby, and now that I'm back, I've been able to help other girls with similar problems. That makes it all worthwhile. I've got the most beautiful baby on earth. Even though I've scarred my life and that of my child, I'm so thankful I listened to you."

Young people, why do I talk about getting out of the back seat of the car and taking a stand with your life and saying no to immoral sex? Because in a period of one day you can make a mistake that will affect your life forever.

I think teenage pregnancy is one of the most serious problems in our society. It's sad when the United States, the most powerful and wealthiest nation in the world, has the highest teen pregnancy rate.

And I think it's about time that we speak up on behalf of that mother who is no more than a child herself. Yes, we have children raising children, and in many cases children are running the home.

A recent study showed that children having children costs our society twenty-nine billion dollars a year. It has simply gotten out of control, and something has to be done.

Why are teenage pregnancies out of control? Simply because everybody wants to be loved, and so many of our children are living in broken homes where they don't feel loved.

And children born to a teen mother come into the world with three strikes against them. Sons of teen mothers are almost three times as likely to end up in prison as other young men. Daughters of teen mothers are eighty-three percent more likely to become teenage mothers themselves. Children born to teen mothers are more likely to repeat a grade in school, they perform significantly worse on development tests, and are twice as likely to be abused or neglected as children born to women twenty and older.

It's high time we take a serious look at this problem and do something about it, because it's affecting our society in a tremendous way.

Young people, don't sell out to immoral sex. Keep your body pure for one man, one woman, for a lifetime, and you will never regret it. Don't look back on your life and say, "If only I had one more chance."

Suicide

I think the saddest people I meet are teenagers. But it doesn't have to be this way. Young people, believe me, each of you has the potential to find real happiness in life. We are all born in darkness, and it's up to each of us as individuals to turn on the light. And we can if only we never give up hope.

Even so, thousands of desperately unhappy American teenagers committed suicide in this country last year. Hundreds of thousands of others attempted suicide. At Georgia State Penitentiary I watched three teenage boys commit suicide. They rolled their bodies right in front of my cell, and I watched them carry the bodies away. And I remember one of them, before he hung himself, he told me from his cell that he was going to take his life. And I've got to live with the fact that I didn't try to help that young boy.

But I cried the day they rolled his body in front of my cell. You know why? Because I was suicidal. I hung on the bars one night to see if my feet would hit the floor. I saw no reason to live. I said, "I can never endure prison life. I can never do these two life sentences. There is no hope for the future. My life is over."

But I'm so thankful that in the darkest hour of my life I made a decision. I made a decision that life is indeed precious. I was going to fight for my life, and that's the reason I'm free today and I'm so thankful for that, young people. You feel many times that there's no hope. No one cares. I know the loneliness you go through. I know the confusion you go through, I know the sexual pressures, I know your vulnerability to drugs and other problems. But no matter what the problem, suicide is not the answer. It is not the answer. And many young people have shared with me their frustrations because they can't communicate with their parents, their teachers, or those in authority. And many have shared with me that they have no one whom they can turn to, but I can tell you that there is someone. And you're going to find out just like I found out that if you'll give your teachers, your parents, and your pastors a chance that they care very much about you. They love you. They don't have all the answers, but they will try to help you. There are a lot of people who care very much about you. Suicide is not the answer.

Many times when I speak in a high school assembly the principal will tip me off to a student who has a very serious problem. At a high school in Georgia, I was told about a sixteen-year-old girl who wanted to commit suicide. The principal called her up to the counselor's office where I met with her for an hour.

"Honey, you're a beautiful girl," I said to her. "Why do you want to take your life?"

"I hate my parents," she answered. "They love my sister and hate me. I'm doing drugs, dating a man who's twenty and having sex." She shook her head and said, "I know it's wrong, but I don't care. Life isn't worth living."

"I want you to know something. I love you very much. Would you do one favor for me? Would you call this number collect when you get ready to take your life? If you do I promise I won't try to talk you out of suicide. I just want to choose the color of the casket, and blue's my favorite color."

She started giggling at my ridiculous humor.

"I can call you collect?"

"Anytime."

Ten days later, on a Friday afternoon in mid-May, she called.

"Mr. Morris, I'm getting ready to take my life."

"Where are you?"

She told me she was sitting in front of a National Guard Armory in a town about sixty miles north of Atlanta.

"I'm leaving right now," I said. "Please give me one hour."

I hopped in my car and drove as fast as I could to the town. I had no idea where the armory was, but somehow I managed to find it quickly. She was sitting on the curb, waiting. She got in the car, and we drove over to McDonald's.

For a while I told her some jokes and made her laugh. I told her about this fifteen-year-old boy who wanted a rifle worse than anything in the world. He pleaded with his mother who rebuffed him. "I told you I'd get you a rifle when you turn sixteen," she said.

Well, the day finally arrived, and his mother bought him the rifle and he immediately went out into the woods behind his house to hunt for a lion. He hunted all afternoon, until it got dark, but he didn't see anything. As he was climbing a hill he suddenly looked up and saw a lion staring down at him. The boy panicked. He threw down his rifle and ran back down the hill as fast as he could, but in his haste he tripped. Laying there on the ground, he heard the lion bounding towards him, and he knew that he was going to be eaten. Just then his mother's words echoed in his memory, "Son, when you're in trouble, pray." So, the boy quickly pressed his hands together and whispered, "Please let this be a Christian lion." Hearing a noise over his shoulder, he looked and the lion was right there. With his paws pressed together in prayer, the lion said, "Please bless this food to the nourishment of my body . . ."

She laughed, and then I told her about the time I was in another restaurant, and I asked the waitress if she had frog legs. The waitress replied, "No, I'm just walking this way because I broke my toe!"

"A mother hen was having trouble keeping her chicks in line," I continued, "and she declared, 'If your father could see you now, he'd turn over in his gravy.'"

After a few more jokes, her face had brightened up and I asked at last, "Honey, what's the problem?"

"I've tried to work things out with my mom, but it's not happening. Yesterday, I saw that man again, and he gave me drugs. I just feel so guilty."

We talked for nearly three hours about her problems. Finally, I drove her home. And we parked in her driveway.

I said, "I'd like to ask another favor."

I pulled some money out of my pocket and handed it to her.

"Will you go and buy something nice for yourself? Then buy a gift for your mother. Sunday is Mother's Day. I want you to give your mom that present and tell her you love her.

"I know you think your mom has failed you. But I'm sure she really does love you. Maybe she just doesn't know how to communicate her love. So you tell her you love her and that you've failed her, too. Say, 'Mom, I want to get to know you and love you.' If you will work at it, the two of you will learn to communicate."

The girl looked at me and then reached over and kissed me on the cheek. With her hand on the door just before jumping out of the car, she asked, "Mr. Morris, who are you? I can't talk to my principal, my teachers, or my parents. But I can talk to you, and I told you things today that I've never told anyone. Who are you?"

There was really only one way to answer her. "Honey," I said, "I'm just a big old ugly ex-con who cares."

That beautiful young girl did not take her life. She gave

up drugs and the twenty-year-old man she was dating. And things gradually improved with her parents, because she learned to communicate and say, "I love you".

Suicide is not the answer.

I'm so thankful I have a burden for young people and for the wisdom to deal with their problems. I know they can mean it when they threaten suicide. I know they can take their lives, even though they really don't want to. Don't tell me a person must be insane to take his life. I once shared that feeling of desperation. There's not a doubt in my mind that I would have fulfilled my intention to commit suicide while I was in prison if I hadn't found hope. I know the feeling of those who want to die, and that has helped me communicate with kids.

Young people know they can share with me because I can keep a confidence. They know that I will do what I say, because my word is my bond. When I tell them I'll write, I write. When I tell them I'll come back, I do. When I give them my card and ask them to call collect, I accept their collect call. That's what they want - someone to understand them, someone to love and accept them as they are, someone to hug them and say, "There's hope, and I love you."

It's high time that we adults realize this. A teenager told me at her school one day she was planning to commit suicide. She said her father had raped her, and although he no longer lived with the family, she still suffered from this grievous emotional wound. I gave her my phone number and asked her to call me so that we could talk further. She did call me, and she also began writing. Her letters were filled with hopelessness.

"I am writing this letter four days after my graduation," she wrote, "and I feel terrible. I have so much pain and hurt eating at me inside that I am about to explode. You know, I still wish I were dead, but I haven't got the nerve to do it - not yet anyway. I just feel so empty and alone.

I'm not happy with myself. I feel so cheap inside about my past. Even though it happened four years ago, the scars are still there. I've tried to put it aside, but something always brings it back. You know, I'm just downright tired of everything.

"Sometimes I wish I had a father who was different. I don't want my real father; I could never love him again. I have forgiven him for what he did to me, but that doesn't change what happened. I can never love him, and I wouldn't let myself even if I wanted to. I just wish I had an adopted father, someone who cares and won't reject me . . .

"I'm so alone. I hope I haven't bored you. Most people who supposedly care really don't . . . How many times I've come to the point of wanting to die! . . . Someone is always better than I am. I feel so rejected at times that if I just blew my head off, very few (I mean very few) people would notice . . . I'm fighting a losing battle. You know, it's pretty lonely . . ."

Could anything make a difference in the life of this desperate teenager? I had to find out. I was determined to become the adoptive father she so desperately wanted and needed. I asked her to tell me something she would really like to do. She wanted to attend a summer camp, so I arranged to sponsor her. With that experience her life began to change. She started singing in the choir in church and seemed hopeful for the first time since we had met.

She indicated that she wanted to come to Atlanta, where I lived, and attend a youth conference. She got to fly on a plane for the first time, and she was just thrilled with the experience. We got to spend some quality time together, and this made a big difference.

I asked if she planned to attend college and even offered to sponsor her. She said she wasn't ready for college yet. However, she did want to study to become a paramedic. So

I sent her to paramedic school, and she later graduated.

Today this young woman who wanted to die is happily married and has a lovely family. She has a bright outlook for the future. Believing in herself and developing her potential made a difference in her life. Young people, please remember suicide is not the answer.

Race

The problem of the 20th and 21st century remains the problem of the color line. This line must, at last, be dissolved. Hardly an aspect of life has escaped this awful thing we call racism.

When I was growing up in South Carolina, many times I heard my father and other adults say that blacks were inferior to whites. They would say that blacks were ignorant, lazy, and smelled bad. Even today, many whites still hold the same beliefs their grandfathers did about blacks, because these beliefs are passed on from generation to generation.

I heard a story from a college professor of mine that illustrates this point. He was at a big international conference in a foreign country. As he talked to a friend of his at the head table, he noticed a well-dressed black man sitting alone at the far end of the table chowing down on a piece of chicken with real gusto.

The college professor said to his friend, "I feel sorry for that black man. He's sitting all by himself, and he probably can't speak any English. Someone really should go and talk to him."

After a few more minutes, the college professor decided that he would go talk to the black delegate. As he approached the black man was still eating, so the professor tapped him on the shoulder. The college professor smiled as he tried to communicate.

"Blah, blah, blah goot?" he said, motioning towards the chicken.

The black delegate stopped eating and looked around for a moment before nodding and responding with, "Goot." Then the black man returned to his meal.

In a few minutes the evening speaker was called, and to the college professor's surprise and chagrin it was the black delegate. Not only did he speak English, but he had an Oxford accent and the most beautiful speaking voice the college professor had ever heard. He gave a wonderful speech that was met with a standing ovation. Stepping back from the podium, the keynote speaker headed towards the college professor, who had his head down until he was tapped on the shoulder. Sheepishly, he looked up.

"Blah, blah, blah goot?" the black man asked.

Sometimes our assumptions are innocent and well-intentioned, but this is where we are today. We still judge people by their skin color, and many whites still feel that those of another color are in some ways inferior. The sad truth is that many fathers have poisoned their childrens' minds with their own hatreds, and society echoes this racial ignorance. Children aren't born racist. They're taught. No wonder our children are confused when it comes to race and many become racists themselves.

On March 21, 1981, in Alabama two young white men, one twenty-six and one seventeen years old, were upset because a black man who had killed a white police officer was found not guilty in a jury trial earlier that day. As part of their Klu Klux Klan Unit 900's "revenge" they set out to kill a black man.

They found a nineteen-year-old black youth walking alone that night, ordered him into their car at gunpoint, drove to a neighboring county, and struck him with a tree limb more than 100 times. When he was no longer moving they looped a rope around his neck and - for good measure - cut his throat.

According to the seventeen-year-old's confession to the F.B.I. and his trial testimony, the two Klansmen then drove back to Mobile County to the home of the twenty-six-year-old's father, who was the second-highest Klan official in Alabama, to show off the trophy to unit members.

They tied thirteen knots in the rope around the black teenager's neck, looped the rope over a branch of a camphor tree on the avenue across the street from the father's home, and let the body swing. There is no question that the young man was trying to impress his father and would not otherwise have done the horrible crime.

On June 6, 1997, the twenty-six-year-old was put to death in the electric chair in Alabama. He was among the rarest breed of Alabama killers: a white sentenced to die for murdering a black. In fact, his execution was the first in the white-on-black murder category in Alabama since 1913.

How tragic! Yes, the sins of the fathers are visited on their children in many instances. The chain of hatreds that has been passed down from parent to child must be broken if we are ever to be free of racism. What our children know and believe, whether it is good or bad, they learned from watching and listening to their parents and those around them.

We must make every effort to be positive role models for our children, and raising our children must become a top priority in our lives. That means teaching children right from wrong, providing loving discipline, and encouraging respect for the dignity and humanity of others. It means teaching each child self-respect. It means being compassionate and caring as a parent and spending time with your children. When you treat a child as if he's worthless, he feels that he can never contribute anything worthwhile to society. Every child should feel that he's a valuable human being.

Too often these days the responsibility for raising the children is left to the mother. After a father deserts the family, you'll find that mother working several jobs if it's necessary. She will do anything and everything she can to support her children. A mother loves in a special way, and she will do whatever it takes to hold her family together. It's mothers that are the backbone of our society - not fathers. And I truly believe that a man is not really a man until he's in touch with the woman in him, and that's why mothers are so special.

But children need their fathers, as this story illustrates:

After I finished a speech in a high school in Alabama one day, a huge black kid built like Hercules came up to me. One of the students had already told me that he was the school's outstanding athlete and was going to a major college on a football scholarship.

In front of the entire student body, he said, "Mr. Morris, you're a great man. I've never had a father, and I was wondering if you would be my father."

Putting my arm around him, with tears in my eyes, I said, "Son, I'm honored you'd want me to be your father. However, I'm afraid I wouldn't do a very good job, because I live in Atlanta, Georgia, and I'm travelling most of the time. But I'll always be available to you. I will always be there for you. You can visit me, call me collect anytime, or write me. I'll help you any way I can. I love you, son, and I'm extremely proud of you."

I then gave him my card, and he gave me a big hug. All he wanted was to be loved and accepted. All he needed was a father's touch. Yes, fathers can make all the difference in the world in a teenager's life.

And I think black men are the ones that the black kids should be looking up to. They must become positive role models for future generations of black youth. Black fathers can provide strong leadership and can solve problems in the black community better than anyone else. Mothers cannot be expected to do it all by themselves - and they shouldn't have to.

But too many black fathers and teens have lost hope for the future. Often they feel that the system doesn't work for them or that it has a bias against them that keeps them in poverty. And as long as we ignore their concerns and needs, we will continue to see more violence and crime. Let's face it, we have created a criminal justice system that only focuses on the symptoms and not on the causes. Building more jails and locking up more young people isn't the answer. Our youth are our responsibility. I think we should spend more time and money training and educating them. They must be taught to achieve, to realize their potential and their talents. Of all the tragedies, I think unrealized potential is the worst.

Racism will not disappear just by focusing on race. Racism will disappear by focusing on achievement and finding a way for every citizen to be an achiever.

I'm convinced that two of the most important issues at the root of racism are education and economic opportunity. Unless we figure out a way to fix our worst schools and open the marketplace to minority businesses so that everyone can see the promise of a better life, the conditions will only worsen as far as racism is concerned.

When we improve our schools, make our neighborhoods safe, and significantly increase the number of minority-owned businesses we put the American dream within everyone's grasp. And it is imperative not that everyone succeed, but that everyone has the opportunity to succeed. The time has come to decide whether our nation will splinter along racial lines - causing us to become increasingly separate, unequal, and isolated - or else become the world's first truly multi-racial democracy. It's imperative that we understand the importance of ethnic and racial diversity to American success.

It is time for all of us to come together and fight for

social and economic justice for all people regardless of color. I believe that we have improved in some cases. Minorities have been given more opportunities. But the situation as a whole has to be improved, because people are still judged by the color of their skin and not by the content of their heart. If we don't make it together, we'll fail separately.

And at present, we are not one nation under God, indivisible, with liberty and justice for all. We are a nation divided between the blacks and the whites. Let's face it, there is not enough respect between the races.

A recent study seemed to confirm the adage that Sunday morning in church-going America is when the nation's racial divide is the greatest. More than 70% of both blacks and whites say they worship where most church members are of the same race as themselves.

It doesn't have to be this way. Where we see differences, God does not. God is color-blind.

Racism has diminished all of the lives it has touched. I think it is high time for all of us, old and young, black and white, to come together.

God is not concerned whether we are black, white, or what color we are. The color of our blood is red.

This was a very difficult lesson for me to learn. I had blindly hated blacks all of my life until one day at Georgia State Penitentiary when the warden threw me into a cell with a black man. His name was Marcus "Doc" Odomes. Through a long and painful process he and I learned to see one another as individuals. I think racism in America exists because the white community, as a whole, has made race a problem from generation to generation. So doing away with racism is ultimately the responsibility of the white community, and I told Doc I was sorry for having hated him. He apologized for hating me. And we became great friends.

You see, our hearts had changed, and once they did we

began thinking and behaving differently. We stood up for one another, and when two white inmates came after me wanting to kill me, Doc didn't hesitate to put himself between me and my attackers. During the ensuing struggle, they stabbed him seven times. After the guards rushed him to the prison hospital, I cried as I looked at his blood. You know why? Because it was red, the same color as mine. Then and there I prayed for him.

Why can't we all learn to love one another like Doc and I learned in that prison cell? Why have we failed as a society in regards to integration? I don't believe that Americans are really interested in telling the truth or in hearing the truth about race. People don't want to change, because change can be difficult. You have to let go of the past and begin to think and behave differently, acting according to your convictions. Even now, I think blacks still feel the pain of slavery, and whites still feel the guilt.

Martin Luther King Jr. first challenged us as individuals and as a nation to act according to our convictions in regards to race more than thirty years ago. But back then we did not take up his challenge. I know I didn't.

On February 27, 1960, I witnessed the very first lunch counter sit-in protest at the Woolworth's in Greensboro, North Carolina. A college student at the time, my college buddies and I cursed those blacks and the few whites who demonstrated with them.

But that demonstration helped to spark the civil rights movement and Martin Luther King Jr.'s dream. What was his dream? He lived and died for equality, truth, peace, democracy, justice, non-violence, and love for all people - regardless of color. He taught that you can never right the wrong of violence with more violence and that no injustice can live forever.

His dream was a glorious one, and even now we are still struggling to realize it as a nation. Hopefully, we can learn to look past the color of the skin, and if we do we will find that we are more alike than different. And then we can begin again to try to communicate with one another, to learn from one another, to understand one another, and - finally - to love one another.

If we can learn to love one another, if each of us can sow just one seed of love into our lives, it may take some time, but the love will come back to us a thousand-fold. The law of the harvest says so.

But we must sow the seeds. We must be the ones who make the effort, because we can't wait on government any longer. The leadership and the commitment must come from each of us, our communities, our churches, City Hall, Boys' and Girls' Clubs, and corporations. And it only takes one person to make a real difference as this story illustrates:

Edwin Tucker, a close friend of mine, led a group of businessmen from Wilson, North Carolina, who wanted to do something for the underprivileged youth in their community. He knew that few if any of them had ever had the opportunity to go to a college football game, and he thought that it would be a treat for them. So, he contacted the local Boys' Club and told them what he wanted to do. He then bought a block of tickets for a football game at the University of North Carolina and arranged to have the children bused to and from the game.

One of those children who got to go to the Tar Heels game on that bright fall day was a thirteen-year-old black boy named Octavus Barnes. Octavus, whose mother and father were divorced, was reared by his grandmother in a housing project. He had never experienced anything like the pageantry or the excitement of being at a big-time college football game. He was thrilled, and he wanted more than anything to be on that field playing before thousands of cheering Carolina fans.

The next Monday he approached the director of the

Boys' Club and asked him, "Do you think I could play for the University of North Carolina someday? It's the most beautiful place I've ever seen."

The director told him, "If you'll apply yourself and work as hard in the classroom as you do on the field you can. You can do anything you set your mind to."

That was all the young boy needed to hear. He starred at receiver on his high school football team and applied himself in the classroom, and he realized his dream of playing for the University of North Carolina.

On August 12, 1997, as he was preparing to leave his home in Wilson, North Carolina, to return to Chapel Hill for his senior year, he told his mother that he had learned from John Lotz, the assistant athletic director of North Carolina, the name of the man who had given him the ticket to his first college football game. Octavus told his mother that he could not return to college without thanking the man.

He went down to Edwin Tucker's furniture store and asked to see his benefactor. When Edwin stepped through the door of his office, the young man extended his hand and said, "Sir, I am Octavus Barnes, and I just wanted to thank you for giving me that ticket. You'll never know how much of an impact it has had on my life. Sir, I will graduate this December with a degree in sociology."

Edwin Tucker congratulated the young man on his success and told him that he was sending another group of inner city youths to the September 6th Tar Heel football game against the University of Indiana. He said that John Lotz had arranged for him to obtain 200 tickets. Octavus said that he'd like to speak to the group after the game.

On the day of the game, 200 youths and Octavus Barnes' mother rode on buses to Chapel Hill, North Carolina, to watch the Tar Heels take on the Hoosiers. The children were given $10 each to spend at the game.

Octavus Barnes started at receiver for the nationally-

ranked Tar Heel football team. He played an outstanding
game and scored a touchdown. After the game, as his
mother and Edwin Tucker looked on, he spoke to the
children.

"I can't tell you what it means to have all of you here.
It certainly brings back memories. Ten years ago, Mr.
Tucker gave me a ticket to a Carolina football game, and
it had a tremendous impact on my life."

Octavus pointed to where he sat in the stands so long
ago, and he told the children how deeply the game
affected him. He related how the director of the Boys' Club
told him to chase his dream of playing football in Chapel
Hill and urged him to work hard on the field and in the
classroom.

"I made a commitment that day to get better in football,
to apply myself in the classroom, and to stay out of
trouble," Octavus said. "I went home after school every
day and studied, and then I went to the Boys' Club. The
Boys' Club kept me out of trouble and on a straight and
narrow path, and it helped me to reach my goal. I will
graduate in December, and I owe my success to the Boys'
Club and to my loving mother and grandmother, who
supported me all the way."

After his speech, Octavus autographed posters of the
Carolina football team for the children. And he thanked
Edwin Tucker for helping him and for helping all of the
kids that surrounded them that day.

"They're all worth it, aren't they?" Octavus asked,
already knowing the answer.

If racism is to be eradicated, the leadership has to come
from us as individuals. And we can all make a difference
if we're willing to plant that one seed.

A young woman once complained to Mother Teresa,
"What am I to do? I'm just one person, and there are so
many people who need help! I can't help everyone!"

Mother Teresa's reply was simple and instructive,

"Then, just help one person."

Little Things

Young people, you cannot compromise with sin. I've tried it, and I can tell you for a fact that it can't be done. You begin by taking just a single step down into the muck and mire of sin, and before you know it you are in over your head.

Take, for instance, cheating on a test. You try to justify the cheating by saying, "Well, last night I talked to my girlfriend on the phone so long I didn't have time to study. I won't cheat anymore."

But then you cheat again on the next test. And on the next one. And before you know it, it's time for the final exam. It counts for half your grade, and it will cover everything you were supposed to have studied all semester. Too late, you realize that you never really knew all of the material, because you cheated on every test. And even though you passed the tests, you'll fail the final exam and you'll fail the class. So, be aware of the little things, because they grow into big ones.

Let me give you the best illustration I could ever use to show you the importance of the little things in your life. Let me tell you about my most unforgettable character. His name was Sheephead.

I had begun to hear tales about Sheephead as soon as I arrived in prison. Inmates and guards spoke of a wild man who was reported to have killed seventeen inmates, and some said he had stabbed hundreds of prisoners during the thirty-odd years he had spent in prison. He had also killed one guard and permanently disabled another.

The story was widely circulated that Sheephead chopped an inmate to pieces with a meat cleaver and flushed the parts down the toilet. The guards thought the man had escaped - until they found his skull. It was too large to flush.

Locked in a wing of the prison to minimize the danger to himself as well as to other inmates, Sheephead became a living legend.

Three years passed before I met him. I was being taken to the outside hospital for surgery after severely injuring the little finger on my right hand in a fight.

A guard said, "Wait a minute. Another inmate is going with you."

The door opened, and there he stood, the man reputed to be the most violent inmate in the prison. I recognized him immediately, because his face did indeed resemble a sheep's head. Every facial bone had been broken in fights. I was frightened of the man.

When the guard shackled my right arm and ankle to Sheephead's left arm and ankle, I worked to steady my breathing so he wouldn't sense my fear.

"What if he tries to escape and both of us are shot?" I thought.

I worried as we were loaded into the prison van for the trip to Talmadge Memorial Hospital in Augusta, Georgia. We rode in silence for a while, and then I found the courage to speak.

"Is it all right if I talk to you?" I asked.

"Yeah," growled Sheephead.

"Are all the stories I've heard about you really true?"

"You ain't heard nothing yet," he boasted, and for 110 miles he poured out the story of his life.

He was from a poor family in south Georgia. As a sixteen-year-old boy he had broken into a store to steal a

Pepsi and a pack of crackers. He was sentenced to one year in Georgia State Penitentiary. Inmates with a one-year sentence are usually paroled in six months and discharged in eight months.

"I had never been in a fight in my life until I came here," he said. "That first day in prison I was raped by an old inmate. My life was never the same after that. I became a homosexual and a drug addict, but I lived for the day I would be released."

Four months after arriving at the prison, the boy was working on an outside farm detail under the supervision of armed guards. Two old convicts forced him to take part in an escape plot: the men would grab a shotgun from one of the guards, and the teenager would seize the gun from the other guard. Fearing the convicts, the boy complied and grabbed the gun as told, but the two other men did not follow through. In self-defense, the boy shot both guards, killing one and paralyzing the other for life.

"When that guard died, I knew that I was through," Sheephead whispered.

For a few moments we rode along in silence before the story continued. After a murder trial, Sheephead was sentenced to die in the electric chair. After he had spent eight-and-a-half years on death row, the governor of Georgia commuted his sentence to life, and he was returned to the inmate population.

No longer frightened, I became fascinated by the old prisoner. As I listened to him and watched him talk, I began to realize that this sick old man was more like a lonely child than a notorious criminal.

When we returned to the prison, Sheephead was locked in a cell in the hospital ward where I worked. Hated by guards and inmates alike, he was a forgotten man. No one cared. He was dying of cancer, although his illness had not yet been diagnosed.

I visited Sheephead daily, often bringing him candy and

a Pepsi. As we talked through the bars, I realized that he was so feeble-minded from being beaten in the head that he would kill an inmate if someone merely suggested the man was out to get him. I suspect this accounted for many of the prison killings.

Others saw Sheephead as a violent animal. But I saw him as a broken man who appeared to be 100, though he was only fifty. He loved me because I didn't look down on him. I gave him time and attention, and he returned the friendship by doing whatever I asked. One day, he told me he was planning to kill the doctor.

"He says I just want to go to the hospital to rest. I know I'm dying, but he won't do anything for me. I'm going to kill him," he said.

He showed me a knife, but didn't explain how he had obtained it. I begged him not to carry out the plan and promised to see that he received proper medical attention. He agreed. I pleaded his case with the hospital administrator, and tests soon confirmed that he had terminal cancer. As I looked at him, tears filled my eyes and I wondered, "Will that be me someday?"

Soon after that Sheephead died, after spending thirty-four years in prison. His unwanted body was buried in the prison graveyard. What began with stealing a Pepsi and a pack of crackers ended in a terrible waste of a life.

You know, the tragedy is not that Sheephead died, but that he never lived. So you can see, young people, how the little things can grow into big ones.

Love

I was at Georgia State Penitentiary for five years, and I never heard the word "love" mentioned. Before leaving Georgia State Penitentiary, I'd made a statement that all I wanted in life was a chance to share love.

Upon my release from prison, I was paroled to the Boys' Home in Orangeburg, South Carolina, where little unwanted, unloved, abused boys taught me the true meaning of love. Now I had my chance. I could become a loving, supportive father to dozens of boys who had no father. In addition, I would be paid a whopping six thousand dollars a year!

When I arrived at the Boys' Home, the boys were waiting for me. Large yellow ribbons were tied around the pecan trees, and a big sign announced, "Welcome home, Mr. Morris." I cried, realizing that here I would be loved and needed. It was one of the most touching moments of my life.

My responsibilities included coaching and counseling the boys who were ages eight to sixteen and from varied backgrounds. Some were orphans, some had been abused and neglected by their parents, some had been kicked out to roam the streets, and some were from broken homes. They were exactly what I needed. Being outcasts themselves, they wouldn't look down on me. I learned a great deal as those kids worked their way into my heart.

One unforgettable eight-year-old really won me over.

Jerry had been abused by his parents. His vision was poor, and he spoke with difficulty. His mental ability also appeared limited, and the kids picked on him constantly. Once, Jerry and several others attended a large summer camp. When I stopped by to check on them, I noticed that all the kids from the other places were eating snacks, but my boys had no money for such treats. I bought them each a candy bar and a soft drink and left some money in an account for each boy. As I started to leave, little Jerry came running up to me.

"Mr. Harold, I know why you bought that candy and pop," he said.

"Why?" I responded.

"Because you love us," he said, wrapping his arms around my legs.

I turned my face so that he couldn't see the tears. That small boy - so physically and mentally limited that he could hardly express himself - was the only boy who showed gratitude. He gave more love than all the others! I have never forgotten Jerry or the lesson I learned from him: never judge a person by what he appears to be; it's the heart that counts. And this little boy, though handicapped, taught me the importance of sharing love and reaching out to others who are less fortunate.

One of my most memorable Sundays was Mother's Day in 1978, shortly after my release from prison. It was special because I was thinking so much about my own mother. For the first time in ten years, I'd be spending Mother's Day with her. After the service, I planned to make the 80-mile drive to her home for dinner that night.

But the day was also special because of Toby, one of the boys who sat next to me. Toby was thirteen and disliked by most of the other kids, because he was starving for attention. He'd have to rank among the greatest liars I ever met, but his fibbing was all done for attention.

Toby was all arms and legs and absolutely pathetic on

the athletic field. He tried to make up for it with big talk and bragging. The other kids resented his mouth and tried to pick fights, but he'd always back off when he was provoked. He was too gentle to be tough. There was a sweetness about him, and he was not afraid to say, "I love you," or "I care". He just needed somebody to love and care for him, too.

One day Toby told me that he never knew his father and that his mother didn't care about him.

"Why wouldn't they care about me?" he asked with tears in his eyes.

"I don't know your parents or why they gave you up," I responded. "But I doubt it had anything to do with you. Parents sometimes act very childish. They want a child but later decide they can't be good parents."

Then I told him that I understood his hurt, "Toby, for nearly ten years I felt no one loved me. While I was in prison, I felt all alone and that nobody really cared."

It hurt me as much as it did him that it was primarily the attractive kids who were invited to the homes of prospective adoptive parents.

So one weekend I told him, "Toby, I'm signing you out today. We're going to the beach. You're going to be my buddy this weekend."

At the beach, Toby had the time of his life. I gave him money for rides and let him eat all the hot dogs and junk food he wanted. He acted like a boy turned loose in a toy store. After that weekend, he followed me everywhere.

And so he sat next to me in the fifth row that Mother's Day Sunday. The pastor presented awards and gifts to the oldest and youngest mothers in the congregation, and then he spoke about how mothers mirror God's love for us. In light of my reunion with my own mother, it was a very emotional message for me.

As I looked around the church, I saw mothers sitting with children in their laps and husbands with their arms draped proudly around the shoulders of their wives. Then I looked at the disadvantaged boys and couldn't help thinking how the pastor's message was being received by their little ears, because they had no mothers.

At the end of the service, Toby got up without saying a word to me and walked down the aisle. The pastor leaned down, and Toby whispered something in his ear. Then Toby turned around, and I could see his lips quivering and tears streaming down his cheeks as he faced the silent congregation.

With a shaking voice the pastor said, "Ladies and gentlemen, little Toby from the Boys' Home has come to us with a very special prayer request. He hasn't seen his mother in more than five years, but he says he loves her very much and prays for her every day. Toby wants to know if we'll pray for his mother — that she's safe and that one day she will love him."

As the pastor led in prayer, the entire congregation was gripped with emotion. When Toby came back and sat next to me, my eyes were flooded with tears. I leaned over, put my arm around his shoulders, and drew his body closer.

"Toby, I can't take the place of your mother," I said, "but I love you and will be a father to you if you let me."

He put his hand on my leg and said, "I love you, Mr. Morris."

I looked him in the eye.

"I love you, too, son," I responded.

It wasn't his fault that his father and mother had deserted him. He needed love, and just as people had reached out and loved me, I could now reach out and love Toby and others like him.

Of course, you don't win them all, and I had my share of failures, too. The most painful involved a blond-haired, blue-eyed boy named Danny. He was nine years old and was everything I could hope for in a son. If boys are made out of snips, snails, and puppy dog tails, little Danny got double of everything. I'd never seen a kid as competitive and tough at his age. He'd fight if necessary, yet he knew how to laugh. He said hip things, walked with a swagger, was built solid as a pit bull terrier, and had confidence that wouldn't quit. He had a smart little mouth, and when I'd call, "Danny!" he'd answer, "That's my name, don't wear it out."

Perhaps because he reminded me of myself at his age, I loved him more than all the other boys. I would have given anything to raise him as my son, love him, educate him, and try to help him become a winner in life.

Endurance was another quality I appreciated, and Danny would never quit. One day I read in the paper about a track meet, so I made special arrangements for the boys from the home to participate in those races. I explained the events to the kids and coached them for a week. On Saturday morning, we hopped into an old van and drove forty miles to Columbia, South Carolina. On the way over there I gave them a little speech.

"If you enter an event, you must finish," I said. "That's all I ask of you. I don't expect you to win, but I do expect you to compete to the best of your ability and cross the finish line. The kids you're competing against are well trained. They're the best in the state. They're already winners, or they wouldn't be here. But, you've been allowed to compete, and you wanted to go - so no half efforts. You finish, and I promise that after the meet I'll feed you all the hamburgers you can eat."

Several thousand people were there to watch the track and field events. All ten kids I brought finished their events, though some of them walked across the finish line. It was pitiful looking at some of them and the way they were dressed. They were anything but athletic, and people laughed at them. I ignored the laughs and worked on the infield, coaching the boys and giving them Pepsi-colas and hot dogs to keep their spirits up.

The last event of the day was the mile run in which
Danny was competing. None of the boys had won any
awards, but I felt Danny had a chance. There were twenty
other competitors in that race, two of whom were rated as
the top runners in the state. One owned the state record for
his age group. As Danny headed for the starting line, I told
him, "All you've got to do is finish third. You'll get a
medal and qualify for the National Junior Olympics. Now
listen to me. It's hot, and you must run four laps around
this track. I'll stay near you here in the infield and help
you pace yourself. Just listen to me."

The gun sounded, and Danny quickly took the lead and
held it through the second lap. The two top runners
caught him, and racing as three they lapped the other
athletes by the final lap. The boy that held the state record
took a one hundred yard lead and finished first. Danny
and the other top runner were neck and neck at the finish
line, but Danny took second by a breath.

I ran to the finish line whooping like a wild Indian and
grabbed Danny. I lifted him up on my shoulders and ran
him around the track. This was more fun than all the
athletic awards I'd won in high school! Danny, an
untrained, uncoached cast off had finished second! I was
crying with joy as I looked up and saw his blond hair
waving in the air and his smile about ready to burst.

When Danny accepted his medal, he took one look at
the prize and turned to me. "One day I'll win the Olympic
gold medal," he said brightly. Since he'd qualified for the
National Junior Olympics, I suggested that we register
immediately.

"I'll pay your fee," I said.

He shook his head, "I can't enter."

"What do you mean?"

"I don't want to be away from the home. My mother
might come to get me, and I have to be there."

I loved Danny so much and wanted to do whatever I

could to help him develop his potential. And I wanted to spare him the heartache of holding onto a dream that I was certain would never come true. Danny's mother had given him up several years before, and I'd never heard of a mother reclaiming her child after that long.

What I really wanted to do was adopt him, but I was prevented from doing that because I'd been to prison and was unmarried. So I figured out an alternative. I went to my brother in Pawley's Island, South Carolina, and I explained the situation. He agreed to adopt Danny, but when I discussed the plan with Danny he objected.

"My mother might come back," he said.

I was disappointed he would pass up the advantages a stable family could offer him. Not wanting to concede defeat to a nine-year-old boy, I invited him to spend a week with my brother's family that summer. My brother had a son two years older than Danny, and together the youngsters had a great time. On the drive back to the Boys' Home, I asked Danny what he thought of my family.

"They're cool."

"Do you like my nephew?"

"He's a little mean, but I straightened him out."

"Well, how would you like to live with them?"

"No thanks."

"But you just said you liked them. They'd be good to you."

"I tried a family once, and I'll never do that again. Nobody cares."

"Listen to me, son. I care. And I'd like to adopt you. You could stay with my brother for now. Once I get married, you can come live with me, and I'll love and educate you. My family will support and stand by you. You can count on me. I'll be loyal to you. I'll give you the life you've never known. I really love you."

Then, without thinking about the potential consequences of what I was saying, I added, "I know this is hard for you to accept, but your mother is never coming back to get you. She doesn't care, or else she'd have returned by now. You've got to give up that dream, son."

Danny looked at me with sudden fury in his eyes. "I hate you!" he sputtered. "You're just like all the others! You don't care! You don't love me! You don't understand! My mother cares about me. She had to make a decision about keeping me or my baby sister, and she gave me away. But she loves me, and one day she's coming back."

"Son, I'm sorry. I didn't mean-"

"I hate you!" he yelled.

"Son, I'm sorry, I'm sorry," I said, with tears in my eyes.

I'd have given anything if I could take back those words, but Danny never forgave me. From that point until the day I left the home, he hardly said ten words to me. No matter what I tried to do, he refused my friendship.

My impulsive response ruined our relationship. But I learned a significant truth: no one can take the place of parents in a child's heart. No matter what happens, a child loves his parents, especially his mother, and he wants to be loved by them. I should have remembered that from my own experiences.

Later, when I visited the Boys' Home during a break from college, I was surprised to learn that Danny's mother finally did return for him. His daddy, whom he never knew, had been killed in a motorcycle accident. There was a will, and his mother needed the boy to collect some insurance money. So she came and got him, and they moved to Texas. After several years I found out he'd dropped out of school and was hanging out on the street. Knowing his toughness, I figured that would happen. It would have been impossible for him to have stayed out of trouble in that environment without proper guidance. It breaks my heart to think he could be in prison now, especially knowing I could have given him the support he needed to make it. I'd love to see him again; I hate to think I might have to visit a prison to do that.

Young people, you may not have much in common with little orphan boys like Toby or Jerry or Danny. But we're all fragile and need to be handled with love.

I believe the word love is the most misused word in our vocabulary. I think one of the saddest things in life is to grow old and be unwanted and unloved.

I'm so thankful there were people who cared for me. They reached out to me when I was a nobody - just convict number 62345. They showed me love. But for every one of me, there are thousands upon thousands who are never loved and end up in nameless cemeteries, like Sheephead Kelly did. And for every little Toby of the world there are thousands of orphan children who never see the face of love, a smile, a kind word, open arms, or an open home.

Children's lives are like twigs. They grow in the direction they are bent. If they are shown love, they grow in love. They become balanced, happy individuals who then, in turn, reach out to others in love.

But if they are abused, ignored, or cast aside, they'll grow in that direction, too. They'll end up hard and bitter. Some of them will end up in prison. Some will end up in a grave without anybody to even claim their bodies. And every last one of us is the same. We, too, grow in the direction we're bent.

Young people, please, won't you tell someone that you love them? Someone needs to hear it as much as you need to say it. You should tell your parents you love them. Now, I realize they will think you're on drugs. Why not go to school tomorrow and tell your teachers that you love them? Tell someone less attractive than you at school that they are special and that you care about them. Now is the time to tell others that you love them.

When I think of wanting to be loved, I'm reminded of the story of a little girl who was orphaned when her parents were killed in an auto accident. She was placed in an orphanage, but she was unattractive and she was teased mercilessly. She had great trouble making friends with the other children. After months of trying, she gave up and kept to herself. One day the director of the orphanage looked out his office window and saw the little girl walking by herself towards the front gate.

Thinking she was trying to run away, the director followed her at a distance so that she could not see him. He watched as she walked through the front gate of the orphanage and down the street to a tree with a branch that stuck out over the sidewalk. She placed a note into the branch and then turned around and walked back to the orphanage.

Later, the director left the orphanage and retrieved the note from the tree. It read, "To anyone who finds this, I love you."

The adolescent years can be years of great selfishness, when young people think only of themselves and would never reach out to someone like a lonely little girl. Reach out to someone who can give you nothing in return or to someone who is unlovable in the eyes of the rest of the world. I believe that we should reach out to others with arms of love. Help little orphan boys like Toby and Jerry and Danny.

Closing

Whatever you do, young people, never forget the things I've talked about. And, in closing, I would like to give you some examples to pattern your life after. You see, I'm not who you want to be in life.

The first example is a twelve-year-old boy who came to the fence at Georgia State Penitentiary and told me that he loved me. When the world had turned its back on me he said, "I believe in you. You're not a murderer." No one believed in me but that young boy.

He told me his name was Jimmy Hale, that his father was a state trooper, and that his mother worked as a nurse at the prison hospital. "We live on the prison reservation," he said, pointing to the white house where he lived. I could see the house from my cell.

He came to the prison fence to see me almost every day. He always wore T-shirts with slogans on them, such as, "I'm a winner! God don't sponsor no losers!" I laughed at his shirts but not at the seriousness with which he shared his faith.

Jimmy always had a basketball in his hands. His goal was to be the greatest basketball player in the whole world, and he was obviously a gifted athlete. We tossed the ball back and forth across the fence. Being a former all-state basketball player, I suggested leg exercises to build his strength and gave him pointers to improve his dribbling. I watched him as he practiced up and down the road and around the guard tower, switching from his left hand to his right and dribbling between his legs.

We developed a strong friendship in spite of the wire barrier. I instructed him about sports and tried to encourage him.

One day, he asked me if I would go to his high school and speak. It was about twenty miles from the prison. I thought he was going to bust me out of the joint.

I said, "How am I going to do that?"

He and his father went to the warden and pleaded their case. Finally, the warden gave in, and I went to his high school to speak. That young boy got up and introduced me and what he said, I'll never forget.

He said, "Students, I want you to know that I care about you. This old man ain't much to look at, but he's my friend and he's taught me a great deal. And I care very much about you, and some of you are wrecking your lives and you know it. You're committing immoral sex acts. You're using alcohol and other drugs. You're going down the same road he went down a long time ago. Please listen to this man. Because forty-five minutes from now he will leave here. He will go back to Georgia State Penitentiary. That door will slam. He will die there. It's real."

The friendship of that little boy helped to make the black days bearable. But I was not prepared for the sad news that he brought me one day. His family had purchased a house in town and planned to move very soon.

"I've brought you something," he said, handing the gift through the fence.

It was a wooden cross he had made using two small branches. He had shellacked them and added a string so that I could hang the cross in my cell.

"I made it myself," he said. "I won't ever forget you, and I want to thank you for teaching me everything."

I said, "I'll never forget you either, Jimmy."

He had become my whole life. Standing there, I didn't

let him see me cry. But after he left I wept.

Then one day his mother, who was a nurse in the prison, came to see me with a special request.

She said, "Tonight his basketball team is in the state finals. The game is going to be on the radio, and he wants you to listen."

Oh, I couldn't wait for the game to get started. He was wearing number 30. My old number. There were five seconds left in the game, his team was down by one, and his team had the ball. They called time-out. They set up one last shot. He took the shot, and made it. He was chosen the outstanding player. He scored 27 points, and they interviewed him on the radio.

In the tense silence that followed, I heard the radio announcer, "We're here with Jimmy Hale whose last second shot won the game. Jimmy, you had a big game with 27 points, and you certainly didn't play like a freshman but you had to be a little nervous when you took that last shot."

"No, sir," Jimmy answered. "I had a good teacher."

That young boy came to that prison to see me the day before I left on parole. Except he was not little anymore. He was a senior in high school, and he could dunk a basketball. He hugged my neck, and he said, "I want to thank you for being the brother I never had."

I said, "I want to thank you for the impact you've had on my life and for loving me."

When you're looking for someone to pattern your life after, young people, I hope you will choose a twelve-year-old boy who had the courage to take a stand with his life - a young boy who dared to be different, who had the courage to stand up to his peer group and say, "Hey, I'm not going to follow you. You need to follow me."

He's the greatest example of positive peer pressure I have ever known. Today, twenty years later, we both live in the Atlanta, Georgia, area. Jimmy has been a state trooper for nearly twenty years and has a lovely wife and three wonderful children. I am godfather to his daughter, Hannah. He remains one of my closest friends, and I'm so thankful that he came into my life.

After all these years, Jimmy is still helping people. On September 1, 1997, he pulled over a car for speeding. The nervous driver was hurrying to the hospital with his pregnant wife, and Jimmy let him off with a warning. Later, Jimmy saw the same black man he had pulled over, William Cody, standing by his car on the side of the road and waving frantically. Jimmy stopped and delivered the baby in the backseat of Cody's car. Later that week the Atlanta Journal/Constitution ran a picture of Jimmy visiting with five-day-old Kiyah Kaitlan Cody and her mother, Tonya, in the Cody home.

The next example is a black man named Marcus "Doc" Odomes, a man I first met at Georgia State Penitentiary.

After the prison rioted, the warden threw both of us into an eight-by-ten foot cell, and the door was slammed shut. In order to successfully integrate the prison, the warden wanted to show that a black and a white inmate could live together. Inmates and guards were laying odds on which of us would kill the other.

Both of us were all-state athletes before entering prison, and we were used by the warden to recruit other inmates to play in the first integrated basketball game in the history of the prison. This game was the catalyst for the successful integration of the prison.

There were only inches of space between the beds in our eight-by-ten foot cell. There we sat, staring at each other.

"You don't like me, do you?" he asked.

"No," I said. "I hate your guts."

He looked at me, and he said, "Why do you hate me?"

I thought I would have had fifty reasons to give him. I couldn't think of one.

"'C-cause you're black," I stammered.

"That's right," he said. "You hate me because of the color of my skin. I don't hate you because you're white. I hate you because you'd be sorry in any color."

To make a long story longer, that man became my closest friend as we spent more than three years in that cell. We shared everything we had. Every time you saw one, you saw the other. The other inmates even called us "Salt and Pepper".

One day two white inmates came to our cell to kill me. Doc fought them in order to save my life. He was stabbed several times and taken to the prison hospital to die.

After they took him away, I cried as I looked at his blood. You know why? Because it was red, the same color as mine.

In the prison hospital, I told him that I loved him and that I owed him my life and would take his place if I could.

"I won't ever forget you," I said. "I won't let anyone forget you. I'll spend the rest of my life trying to teach others what you have taught me."

He squeezed my hand, and in a low, soft, pained voice he said, "I love you, Super Honky. You're a true friend."

Through his life he issued a challenge to me that will go with me to my grave; he challenged me to share what he and I learned in that cell with others. You see, he helped me become free not only from my physical prison, but from the shackles of sin and despair. He shared love with me when I had no one else, taught me how to be color-blind, stood with me when I needed a friend, taught me about faith, and — finally — he was willing to give his life that I might live. His life challenged mine. I shall never forget him. He will forever live in my memory.

In the summer of 1997, I returned to the prison grave-yard, Pissant Hill. As I stood at Pissant Hill in the driving rain, I said, "You were right, Doc. I'm unshackled. I'm free. Freer than I've ever been in my life."

If ever there were young people to say no to all these things that I have talked about, I hope it will be you — this generation. You can make a difference.

I hope that you will remember the importance of making the right choices in your life. And I hope that you will never forget this: you always reap what you sow in life.

FOR GENERAL ORDERING

ALSO AVAILABLE BY HAROLD MORRIS: *Unshackled*

The Law of the Harvest is taken from the novel *Unshackled* by Harold Morris. *Unshackled* is the unforgettable story of two men. One, Harold Morris, was white — a sharecropper's son from South Carolina. The other, Marcus "Doc" Odomes, was black — raised by his mother in inner city New York. Both were doing life sentences in Georgia State Penitentiary when the prison was forced to integrate under federal mandate. It was the last prison in America to do so. They were thrown into an eight-foot by ten-foot cell and the door was slammed shut. Through this gripping story of two men's lives we see how hatred and racism were overcome, and we see the prejudice, pain, suffering, and the thread that binds us all.

Twice Pardoned, the award winning video by Harold Morris, is a 33 minute presentation in which he speaks to 12,000 teenagers about the law of the harvest — a simple truth that applies to the physical as well as the spiritual universe: you always reap what you sow. In this gripping narrative, he discusses wrong association and peer pressure, alcohol, drugs, sex and dating, suicide, race, and the importance of love. He vividly illustrates the crucial importance of making the right choices early in life.

TO ORDER: *Unshackled*: US $24.99/CAN $32.99
                  The Law of the Harvest: US $6.99/CAN $9.99
                  Twice Pardoned video: US $19.99/CAN $27.99
                  OR, all three of the above in one package for
                  US $44.99/CAN $62.99 (a savings of 22%)

Send your order complete with shipping address and check or money order to: **Nantucket Publishing**
                  602 S.W. Ward Blvd.
                  Wilson, N.C. 27893

Please include US $3.99/CAN $6.99 for each individual item (US $4.99/CAN $8.99 for the 3 part package) for shipping and handling; VISA and Mastercard welcome. Sorry, no COD's.

Or visit us on the web at:
www.unshackled.com